TRANS
TIME & SPACE:

HYPNOTIC
TIME
DISTORTION

("ADVANCED HYPNOSIS"
OBE / NLP)

By
Jeffrey Hammer

ISBN #0970271751

P.O. Box 314
Oceanside, NY 11572

Index

Outline

Judgment is set.
Memories of past lives
Yes, we have lived before!
Heaven keeps score!
Creating the out-of-body experience
A meditation
The out-of-body experience

Outline: Part II NLP

The mind "senses" how people process/communicate and understanding language
visual processing:
visual words
visual phrases
visual sentences
auditory processing

auditory words
auditory phrases
auditory sentences
kinesthetic processing
kinesthetic sentences
sensory specific words
unspecific sensory predicate
words
generic speech specified!
The senses:
Primary & secondary processing
Models of people's perceptions
Natural abilities
"Eye" picture processing

Outline: Part III

"Time verbs!"
verbs which show existence

verb forms./list
present/past
"More" time verbs
"Place" verbs
Presuppositions/Assumptions
Assume/Presuppose
Actual/Factual
Permanence
Temporary
Change of state
submodalities
senses
shifting "space"
verbs & prepositions!
A story
(use of the language)
planning the future
time phrases/words
presuppositions of time

time & space words

Part IV

Hypnotic Time Distortion
1) Remodeling
2) Picturing
3) Imagining
4) Steps to a possible future
5) Deviations!
6) Mental processes/trance words
7) Examples/uses of "time distortion"

Part 1

"To be" or "not" to be! "Be" defines "existence"!

I "think" therefore "I am"! "Existence" is again defined!

When I first learned "hypnosis" I would also cross reference definition as "in" hypnotic definitions with an ordinary dictionary. (The best dictionary I could find!)

"Exist": defined is 1) "to be" 2) live! 3) to have "being"!

My definition is for your essence to take: "physical form!"

We as individuals are from a very young age taught to conform! As in "obey" and "comply"! As people leave college or simply enter the work force we are told to be "yes" men and women!

By "questioning" things or "certain things" we raise issues, we look for answers! As we look for answers by raising questions, we begin to want and expect to get them!

"Physical form" means we are born into this world and one day we will "die" as in cease to exist in "physical form" as we know it at this point in time and leave this world!

This life in this form is temporary. People being born into the United States in the year 2002 can expect to live about 120 years!

I can honestly say this because I do palmistry! Palmistry allows me to look at life lines! Most if "not" all of the people who I look at the hand (inside hand) or palm of, have long life lines meaning, if they do "not" do something either stupid or incredibly stupid as in endanger their lives, they will live very long lives!

There is also a very rational reason for this as well! For those of you who do not believe in palmistry or "don't" believe in it yet, we do expect medical advances and innovations will definitely expand the ability of people to live longer.

We expect cures for heart

disease, artificial internal body parts, to replace pumps.

We also expect advances in science for lung and liver diseases, possible advances in science for artificial parts to replace hearts, lungs, and livers, and other internal body parts. Just as "artificial arms and legs," exist today!

Physical Form!

To take up space and exist in time! "100 years" of life, seems like a long time! It is still temporary existence! "Suicide" is "not" an option. Suicide is "failure" as in "absolute failure!" It is a curse that will "haunt you".

Never an escape! You will be punished, as in your "soul" will be punished!

Maybe some of the people reading this are still questioning palmistry, and I now "touch" on 1) the soul (essence), and 2) the subject of reincarnation.

It's not as simple as all "souls" or all "good souls" go to heaven! The road to hell is also paved with good intentions!

People born into life make choices! Choices based on who they are! Belief systems! We define "good" and "bad"! A simple example! The Soviet Union was the United States "ally" during World War II. In 1950's during the

Cold War they were the U.S.'s enemy because of communism and Germany and Japan were the United States allies! The Soviet Union lost the most resources helping the United States beat Germany during World War II (human lives). The example, just given is known by another name "mind control" (brain washing)!

To restate the above example Russia expended the most resources to win World War II against Germany!

By resources I mean human resources/ human lives! People sacrificed their very existence (lives) to defeat Germany! Men who were 17 years old during

World War II in Russia who survived the war year's later are "rare"! As in scarce! A whole generation was sacrificed for the "greater good!" A sacrifice worth remembering!

During World War II there was another war taking place, a war of "evil" vs. "good". Hitler was aligned with Satan/devil and demons and absolute evil!

What Hitler failed to understand was as he killed people the ranks of G-d's angels swelled to the point that Hitler evil demons lost the contest and Hitler lost the war. The war was over at Stalingrad! The war was over at "Midway" in the Pacific! It was decided!

Good and evil exist in the world. Some will even say that "good essence" enters human form (birth) through a good "door" and exits life through a good "door". While evil essences enters through an evil "door" and exits life, also through an evil "door". The thing is while there are two doors a soul only enters and leaves through one door! Good people enter through the good door and leaves usually the same way! Evil enters through the evil door and also usually leaves the same way. What decides the outcome of which door people leave through, is the events and deeds, done in human form on earth. Yes, an evil person can do great good on earth, and a good person born into the world can do great evil! G-d does, judge and heaven does keep score! Heaven keeps score for everything that is done.

At the same time, a number of people say everything is "preordained." Events in some cases do repeat themselves at different points in time! The saying that if we fail to learn from the past we are condemned to repeat it. This theory might hold some truth.

Another theory of time "holds" that as we look back further into the past or attempt to predict things further into the future we are looking at one version of past events or predicting one possible future! Read that last theory again! One possible past, or version of events. A possible recorded history or theory of events (might exist).

The last theory is a "remote viewer theory", theory that people, if given a set of coordinates can travel to the actual place or event of the coordinates and observe the event in a "like" out of body experience form! The U.S. Government kept transferring this program from one government agency to the next until they finally did away with the program, altogether! The reason being is "remote viewing", was considered a "nut" program. No agency wanted to be associated with a program in which a certain segment of the population considered a total waste of taxpayers' money and a crazy program! So the program of remote viewing ended.

I once attended a lecture on out-of-body experiences. The lecturer said that we as humans ascended into human form, from lower beings. Originally saying that we evolved from "one celled" or one atomed entities! Our souls took human form and in our present lives we are even now developing into higher beings! Another lecturer I heard stated that he has the ability to do out-of-body experiences and speak with his guardian angel! A women who I met a number of years ago was very visual. I met her in a club. She told me she would come to me in a dream. She kept her word!

This woman had the ability to have out-of-body experiences. The ability to have out-of-body sex with someone was an absolute turn-on to her. Yes, you are able to have out-of-body sex or "astral sex" with someone! The rules are both participants must agree (willing to participate). I was very attracted to this particular woman and she liked the way I looked and loved the way I danced with her! She had a very nice personality, and was pleasant! Now, I know a lot of men and women will attempt to do out-of-body experiences based on the information I just communicated! For women, they might view astral sex as "safe sex!" Men will now view a "no" now as a "let's see for sure!"

There are numerous reasons beside "sex" to do out-of-body experiences. Numerous books exist on the subject. People will to a lesser extent view you as being a little "off the wall", if you tell them or talk to them about this subject.

I have met simply to many individuals who do out-of-body experiences and read numerous books on the subject. The people who I spoke to and the stories I have read have communicated many interesting things about the out-of-body experience which I will share now!

As stated before, the beautiful Russian blonde woman gave me my first encounter with people who do "out-of-body experiences." "Astral sex" is a wonderful experience. As wonderful an experience as astral sex is, it is only one of many reasons to have an out-of-body experience! The other main reasons are 1.) to communicate with a person in the dream state in this type of setting you may influence the communication, setting, and formality of the communication based on your creativity and imagination. This can be done with a friend, relative, acquaintance, etc. 2.) You can even visit someone halfway around the world! 3.) Children, especially small children, have a natural ability to have out-of-body experiences numerous children "talk" about the famous "falling dream", spiraling down a "hypnotic circle"! Falling down or gliding down the "birth tunnel" or "tube" to be born into human form! A lot of children reflect on being born into the world and do not understand the dream of spiraling down as an unborn soul into human birth.

Before I continue with reasons why to do out-of-body experiences, I would like to state that the human soul experiences "life" and "angel-like form" at different points in time! The process is 1) birth; 2) death; and 3) spiritual growth in life and "after life"; 4) the next process is another incarnation into human form if the souls are deserving of one. (The alternative if the person did absolute evil and is in purgatory and "pain"!)

In at least one of the books I read there was a story about a man who was a homosexual and was in great pain from HIV/AIDS, which he received from his lifestyle. The story further went on about this homosexual man who committed suicide to escape the path of AIDS. In life, we are given a set of circumstances and we are judged for our actions! "Suicide" is "not" an option. It, in fact, makes things worse!

The homosexual man wanted to escape the pains of AIDS which was the reason he committed suicide! He was born into a "new more painful suffering situation" as a "newborn baby with AIDS". An even more painful situation than the last existence, and as an AIDS baby died of AIDS also! (A punishment).

Judgment is set! The soul is either punished in life or death, or the next life! We as people are obligated to accept our births, circumstances, existences and overcome obstacles that enter our lives! We have an obligation to do so as a growing experience for ourselves and our souls! We have to do things in life for ourselves and our loved ones!

When I wrote my first book "Mind Reading in Written Form!" I made the book first in booklet form. I was looking to get it published, and I attended numerous lectures/seminars. I attended two classes in palmistry. In the first class, the man who taught the palmistry class had a turn out of, naturally, mostly women!

This man knew and revealed things not only about my present life by looking at my hands (palms) but also about past lives and my future. Just like the marks and strokes of someone writing is the key to their mind (brain), the lines and marks on a person's hands gives you the road map of their life and possibly their soul! The other interesting things this man did was 1) out-of-body experiences and 2) he spoke with his guardian angel. This man was "awesome" to be able to do that. He was able to go anywhere and visit anyone. This is the secret of the out-of-body experience. You are able to travel anywhere, to your favorite vacation spot or the dark side of the moon!

The reasons why people do not have out-of-body experiences are: 1) In the mist there are "things". Just as angels exist, so do demons; 2) People put blocks so as "not" to have out-of-body experiences in order to protect themselves! 3) The most serious reason why people do "not" do out-of-body experiences is there is a "cord" which connects the soul (astral body) to the human form body. If the line (cord) gets severed, you "die"! People in human form, love life for the most part and wish to live. They also prefer the "3 dimensional" world rather than the "4th" or "5th" dimensional existence.

I met a woman who goes into the "mist" (out-of-body) and said to me she is always pushing "things" away from her. What these "things" in the mist do is drain energy from her. They feed on your energy. The awesomeness of the out-of-body experience and her desire to be there keeps her returning to it! (Escaping human concerns).

Yes, we have lived before. After taking my first class in palmistry, I took a second class on the subject.

The woman who taught the class studied "voodoo" under a Master in the subject. In the class she spoke of hands being classified around the 16th century. She knew for the most part that "exceptional" people had for the most part attended her seminar when she looked at the hands of the people in the room, and also my hands. She was happy that she knew me from a past life. She knew me from my last past life. We were both Jewish in our past lives during World War II. I saved Jewish lives. She betrayed the people of her own faith for her personal life (She did "not" tell me this. I found this out from another individual who made an effort to "meet me").

The woman who did palmistry was given a Roman Catholic Italian incarnation in this life, but she told me she feels a tremendous connection with the Jewish people and the state of Israel. She did "not" explain our relationship in this past life. (I was trying and succeeding in saving lives, and she was interested in saving her own life!) She is now doing a form of service in this life for the deeds of a past life. Heaven keeps score! "Oh" how heaven keeps score! There is a book of records of all things done in life! Things which you find yourself ashamed of in death.

There is a person who lives life with the following motto: "There's no such thing!" He is totally wrong. Heaven judges and keeps score. Anything you do to someone else will happen to you! Life is a growing experience. You get the opportunity to break the chain and end the cycle of repeating the same events in each incarnation on earth. You get the opportunity to "grow" on a human and a spiritual "level". But, as always, the choice is yours!

To create an out-of-body experience, different books and different people will make certain suggestions!

I even heard a meditation by a primarily auditory processor who knew some hypnosis. As he described it to me, he did not use "hypnotic language" but he did some hypnosis. Naturally, I "resisted". I wrote a book on basic hypnosis. Had he used actual hypnotic language, I would have interrupted, deflected and distracted and used language on an even more powerful level! But, this was "not" the case. He was showing me a method, teaching and helping me learn! I will "not" communicate what he said in the way he said it! (He communicated it in hypnotic meditation form).

The basis on this meditation is to "relax". To relax your mind and body!

How he went about it was to ask you to 1) picture a transparent glass table; 2) the table is naturally outside; 3) it is a bright clear sunshining day; 4) the light of the sun is passing through the table. Note: The "light" is the important aspect in setting up the meditation. You want the sunlight to 1) totally energize you and 2) totally energize your body and totally energize your energy body!

Parts of the meditation are: the table is covered with all the things in your life. You want to "clear" all the items on this table, which are blocking the light so you mentally clear the table to let all of the light shine through. The idea is to put everything aside so you can now totally energize yourself!

People who are primary visual processors usually accomplish the out-of-body experience by visualizing themselves leaving their bodies while people who are primarily auditory processors primarily "vibrate" out of the body to have the out-of-body experience. Numerous books contain methods to obtain the out-of-body experience using various methods!

Some books, tapes auditory or even video hypnosis can be used to induce sounds, vibration or visual effects which can help you experience the out-of-body experiences. It's "time" to return to the main subject of the book which is NLP/HYPNOSIS particularly "time" and "space" language. Let's begin with "senses."

PART II
The Senses!

People process, communicate and understand in different ways! While I will "not" communicate in terms of "models of the world" meaning an individual's model of the world, I will communicate in general about how people process, communicate and understand language!

Now, as humans, we have five senses! We 1) see, 2) hear, 3) touch, 4) taste, and 5) smell. On a mental level, we might have an enhanced ability to smell or taste, but on a primary level, we will process the world in one of only "3" ways based on our senses. We as humans are either 1) visual, 2) auditory or 3) kinesthetic processors of language. (Note: kinesthetic refers to "touch" / "feel" language (feelings).

What this means is, if a person is a "visual" processor and communicator, this person will picture things. To be clear and to the point, with this person, you will want to use a lot of visual language. when this person remembers things, they will most likely picture (picture them). When this person thinks they will most likely also (see) picture(s).

If this person wanted to write a book, they would probably run a "movie" in their head (mind).

I usually can tell who is a visual processor by the way light reflects off this type of person's eyes!

As someone who wrote three books on handwriting analysis, I can also tell by looking at one sentence of writing in script of the person's writing if they are visual.

Visual processors of language will use words and vocabulary heavy with visual language and loaded with pictures and colors! Visual individuals are creative, have dreamy like qualities and great imaginations!

Visual language includes the following words: see, look, image, imagine, symmetry, eye-to-eye, brilliant, sights, bright, light, clear, flash, lighting, perceptive, glaring, focus, glimpse, shadow, blur, blank, blind, view, appear, show, dawn, reveal, envision, vision, illuminate, twinkle, clear, fog, foggy, focused, hazy, spark, sparkling, crystal clear and picture.

In using language visual individuals will communicate using phrases such as: "An eyeful", "Appears to me", "Beyond a shadow of a doubt", "Birds-eye view", "A view", "A glimpse of", "Clear cut", "Eye to eye", "See the light", "Looks like", "The big picture", "In the mind's eye", "Plainly see", "Of vision", "A view to a . . . etc."

Now, some more visual phrases and sentences.

1. I see your point (point of view)

2. I wish to have (take) a second look.

3. You can see I'm painting a clear picture.

4. Beyond a shadow of the doubt this is the truth!

5. What you're saying appears pretty hazy to me.

6. It appears to be dim in perspective.

7. The image (focus) of life appears to be crystal clear and sparkling.

Auditory processors will use language: words, phrases and

sentences with sound, hearing and listening words in them! Auditory individuals are usually people who are more detailed, study facts and invest the time to study these facts! Auditory processors of information will be more cautious and detailed as well as analytical and investigative. In handwriting they will write smaller than visual processors, make closer dots to the small letter "i" and round the top portion of letters like: the small letters "m & n". At the bottom portion between the letters between the letters between the humps will be a "v" like mark in the letters. Also note: "light" will usually "not" shine off the eyes of auditory processors. Auditory Processors will use words/phrases including the following: hear, listen, sound, tell yourself, harmony in tune, in rhythm, loud, resonant, static, good ear (any word relating to ear/ears), whisper, echo, silence, deaf, make music, harmonize, tune in/out, I'm all ears/be all ears, ring a bell/ring my bell(s), be heard, resonate, overtone(s), and questions.

Auditory phrases include: afterthought, blabbermouth, clear as a bell, clearly expressed, call on, describe in detail, earful, express yourself, give an account of, grant (you) an audience, voice, voice an opinion, hidden message, hold your tongue, idle talk, inquire of/ inquire (into), loud and clear, manner of speaking, pay attention to, power of speech, purr(s) like a kitten, outspoken, state your purpose, tattletale, tell the truth, tongue-tied, unheard of, well informed, within hearing, word for word.

Auditory sentences can include the following. I hear what you are saying. I want to make this loud and clear. Does what I'm saying sound right to you? The information is accurate, word for word. Does that ring a bell. That seems to resonate with me. It seems to be in perfect harmony.

Kinesthetic words include the

following: feel, touch, grasp, place yourself, balance, solid, hard, bumpy, intuitive (curious), grip, take, put, get hold of, slip through, catch on, catch up, catch up on, make contact, touch base, turn around, get a handle, solid, concrete.

Kinesthetic phrases include: All washed up, boils down to, chip off the old block, come to grips with, control yourself, (cool, calm & collected), on (have a) firm foundation(s), floating on thin air, get a load of this! Get in touch (with!), get the drift of (get the jest of), hand in hand, hang in there, hold on! Get hold of, hot head, know how, lay the card(s) on the table, light-headed, pain in the neck, pull strings, sharp as a tack, smooth operator, so-so, start from scratch, stiff upper lip, stuffed shirt, underhanded, high handed manner.

Kinesthetic sentences will include words relating to feeling and touch. Sample sentences are as follows. He is the person you should touch base with. I feel that this is the way it should be. The information I am communicating is solid as a rock. I'm not following what you are saying. This is exactly what it boils down to. Life can feel wonderful!

The following is a word list to take a second look at what was just communicated:

List of primary sensory specific words:

Visual	Auditory	Kinesthetic
see, look	hear, listen	feel, touch
image	sound	grasp
imagine	tell yourself	place yourself
symmetry	harmony	balance
eye to eye	in tune	solid
perceptive		intuitive, grasp
		grip

Visual	Auditory	Kinesthetic
focus	tune in	go with the flow

Let's take a third look at the sensory predicate words with a column for unspecified words:

Unspecified	Visual	Auditory	Kinesthetic
sense	see	hear	feel
experience	look	listen	touch
understand	view	sound(s)	grasp

The following is a list of sentences based on generic sentence is first.)

Generic:
I understand you.

Visual:
I see your point.

Auditory:
I hear what you are saying.

Generic:
I want to communicate this to you.

Visual:
I want you to see this.
I want you to look at this.
I want you to take a look at this.

Auditory:
I want to make this sound clear.

Kinesthetic:
I want you to get the grasp of this.

Generic:
Are you understanding what I am communicating?

Visual:
Am I painting a clear picture?

Auditory:
Does what I'm saying sound correct?

Kinesthetic:
Are you grasping the situation?

Genetic:
I know that to be true.

Visual:
Beyond a shadow of a doubt that's the truth.

Auditory:
Word for word that's correct.

Kinesthetic:
This information has a real solid foundation.

Generic:
I'm not sure about that.

Visual:
It appears a bit hazy to me.

Auditory:
That doesn't really ring a bell.

Kinesthetic:
I'm not following you!

Generic:
I don't like what you are doing.

Visual:
I view what you're doing with a negative perspective.

Auditory:
That does not resonate well with me at all.

Kinesthetic:

I don't feel right about what you're doing.

Now, I will go into the theory of the "human mind".

We have "5" senses. (Not counting the "sixth sense"). I am referring to our senses of: 1) sight; 2) hearing; 3) touch; 4) taste; and 5) our ability to "smell". Our minds are based on the first "3" senses of 1) sight; 2) hearing; and 3) touch. Also known as our abilities to see, hear and touch (feel). The following charts will be based on how people perceive.

People process information on one of several different ways based on how their minds work. The following six charts are all "original". People perceive on a primary level, secondary level and on a third level. The primary level, makes the person good at certain tasks, the secondary level reinforces the primary level. The third level will tell you what the person is least likely to excel in.

<u>Model 1</u>:
<u>Primary Visual Processors</u>:
Primary level: visual
Secondary level: auditory
Third level: kinesthetic

Model 2:

Primary level: visual

Secondary level: kinesthetic

Third level: auditory

Primary Auditory Processors

Model 3:

Primary level: auditory

Secondary level: visual

Third level: kinesthetic

Model 4:

Primary level: auditory

Secondary level: kinesthetic

Third level: visual

Primary Kinesthetic Processors

Model 5:
Primary level: kinesthetic
Secondary level: visual
Third level: auditory

Model 6:
Primary level: kinesthetic
Secondary level: auditory
Third level: visual

In theory, the "model 3" processors are usually the most powerful group, in terms of: powers and abilities (auditory, visual, kinesthetic processing.)

The second most powerful group in theory is the: "Model 1" processors. The visual, auditory, kinesthetic processors have a natural ability to visualize themselves out of their bodies.

People who process auditory on a primary level are natural language learners. Even if people process on a secondary level, they can still be good language learners.

People who process auditory primarily have a natural ability to remember the way things are "said" and "how" they were said, especially if the person is a good listener.

Visual primary processors lean more toward "art" and "design", just as auditory processors lean more toward "language" and "music".

Kinesthetic primary processors will lean usually toward: "writing", and jobs with: travel positions and figuring things out!

People who "visualize" either on a primary or secondary level have creative abilities.

People who visualize least might be "accident" prone. (If you are in this category should be more observant when in movement (walking/driving, etc.) Again, the level 1 and level 3 individuals will have the easiest time doing "out-of-body experiences"!

1. visual construction

Human Processing

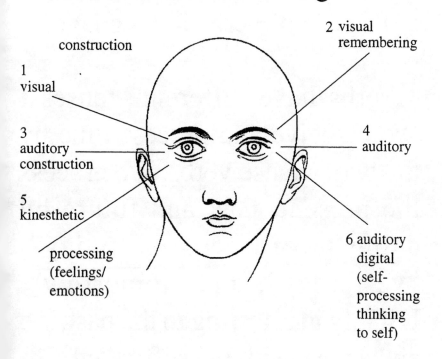

1 visual construction

2 visual remembering

3 auditory construction

4 auditory

5 kinesthetic processing (feelings/ emotions)

6 auditory digital (self-processing thinking to self)

2. visual remembering
3. auditory construction
4. auditory remembering
5. kinesthetic processing of feelings/ emotions
6. auditory digital processing (thinking to oneself).

Time Verbs!
The use of verbs in language!

Verbs have different "tenses". We perceive and process time by the way we use verbs. We process the present, past and future by using words like "today", "yesterday", and "tomorrow". Usually in referring to the past, we end a verb with the suffix "ed". In talking about he future, we talk in terms of something that "will" occur! Example: "I will succeed tomorrow!" or This "shall" happen!"

There is a group of individuals that have difficulty with the concept and/or pasting of "time".

Time does "not" stand still! Our perception of time allows us to exist in "3" dimensional forms, on earth and in life. We exist, take up space and exist as "time" passes!

Language is presented to communicate past events, present events, and future events!

The definition usually given for a "verb" is: A "verb" is an action word! Verbs are move than "action words!" Verbs can be helping words (verbs) and linking words (verbs). Verbs can show existence such as the linking verbs: be, an, is, seen, appear, believe, was, were, remain, etc.

To communicate the past, as in the past or the past perfect: "d" or an "ed" is usually added to the verb. The rule with the future/ future perfect is a helping verb is usually added to an existing verb to show future (understanding) of time.

The following is a partial list of 1) present; 2) past; and 3) past participating "verbs"! (Note: past participating verbs need a helping verb).

Verb Forms

Present	Past	Past Principle
bear (carry)	bore	borne
begin	began	begun
bend	bent	bent
bite	bit	bitten
break	broke	broken
bring	brought	brought

catch	catch	caught
choose	chose	chosen
deal	dealt	dealt
dig	dug	dug
dive	dived	dived
do	did	done
drag	dragged	dragged
drink	drank	drunk
fall	fell	fallen
feel	felt	felt
fly	flew	flown
forget	forgot	forgotten
freeze	froze	frozen
get	got	gotten
give	gave	given
go	went	gone
grow	grew	grown
hang	hung/	hung/
	hanged	hanged

have	had	had
lie	lied	lied
light	lighted, lit	lighted, lit
ring	rang	rung
ride	rode	ridden
run	ran	run
sing	sang	sung
speak	spoke	spoken
steal	stole	stolen
swim	swam	swum
take	took	taken
wear	wore	worn
weave	wove	woven
write	wrote	written

Now, for advanced hypnosis as in" Change of Time Verbs and Adverbs", words such as the following are used in "hypnotic" language!

Change of Time Verbs and Adverbs:

Begin

End

Stop

Start

Continue

Proceed

Already

Yet

Still

Anymore

(Note: space is left to write in dictionary definitions and/or group "Similar" usable words, or your definition for word!)

Change of Place Verbs!

come

go

leave

arrive

depart

enter

Rules: Presuppositions & Assumptions"

Presuppositions: Are "assumptions!" Note: Assumptions can be "wrong"!!! Things we assume to be true make sense! What is assumed to be true makes sense to us. Presuppositions are what must be "assumed"!

Presupposition are not necessarily directly stated! When

we talk, usually we talk in terms
of something that has or will take
place. Something or an event that
we understand to be "true" or the
"truth". We presume or presuppose
as in "accept to be true!"

The following words and
phrases "Presuppose!"
automatically
continuously
spontaneously
even without thinking
second nature
steadily
instinctively
almost magically
constantly
involuntarily
unconsciously

(Note: room left for synonyms/ definitions).

Note #2: (Notice: most of these words end with the letters "ly"!)

To presume that something is "true", "actual" and/or "factual"!

List of words which presuppose "truths!"

absolutely
actually
genuine
evident
real
really
true
truly
obvious
obviously
factual

fact
proven
verified
valid
certainly
positively
definite
definitely
positive
sure thing
clearly

Note #1: Space left for definitions/synonyms.

Note #2: Notice most words end with "ly".

The following is language which presumes "permanence!"

last
lasting
remain
remaining
persisting
long standing
ending
unending
year after year
timeless
end
endless
without end
non-stop
continually
continuously
fixed
ongoing
going on and on

goes on and on
staying with it
stay with it
enduring
staying power
staying
persistent
long term
forever
everlasting
endless
constant
perpetual
always
never ceases
continue
continuing
stable
long lasting

extend
extending
day after day
week after week
month after month
year after year
eternal
never ending
always
ceaseless
in perpetuity
secure
keeps on
keeping on and on

Note #1: The above language presumes permanent

Note #2: "Nothing" is permanent!

Note #3: Now that you know language that communicates permanence, be careful with it! You could get into "trouble" if used wrongly!

Note #4: Space was left next to each word for definitions/synonyms

Note #5: Notice most words indicating "permanence" end with the suffix "ing"!

Since "nothing is forever" in human life, maybe you wish to use language which communicates that things are "temporary prepositions"!

The following list of words and phrases that imply a limitation of "temporary"!

temporary
for a while
fade away
fade like a shadow
up in smoke
in a puff of smoke
go up in smoke
short-term
in a second
in a blink of an eye
change immediately
in nothing flat
at the speed of light
replaceable
replaced by
change with the times
changes with the time
changes with the times
stop

brief
in an instant
stop for a second
pause
like a dream
vanish like a dream
melt away
vanish
melt like snow
fading
like a fading memory
vanished
put in place of
change one's mind
final
changeable
in no time
no time
no time for

burst
bursted bubble
burst like a bubble
here today
gone tomorrow
here today, gone tomorrow
for a short time
disappear
just disappear
just disappeared
momentary
momentarily
in no time
evaporate
evaporated
terminate

Note #1: The above language presumes temporary.

Note #2: "Nothing" in life is permanent.

Note #3: Space was left for synonyms and definitions.

Marriage is till "death" does us part! The great equalizer is "death". As in we "part this earth"! Then we get judged in what we did in life!

Examples:

Things as well as people can be "short lived" as in "temporary"! which forces "limitations" as in "changes"! In an "instant" things or people can be "replaced"!

The above was how temporary presuppositions are used.

In science, if we talk about H_2O,

we can refer to the liquid, the solid or the gas of water as in changes of "state". In language, the words we use to describe how things take up space or change their state is called "change of state verbs!"

List of change of state verbs:
change
transform
turn into
become

Now I attended "2" psychic conventions. The first as a speaker, because I am an author of three handwriting analysis books. I read cards, and I do some palmistry. Mostly, however, my ability is reading writing, which is a natural ability! At the first convention, I asked the audience how many "senses" they have. Some did "not" know. Others said "6" as in a sixth sense and some said "5"! As in actual senses!

Submodalities are about information which we gather by the use of our "5" senses. In NLP our "5" senses are called our representation system or "modalities"

List of "5" senses:

vision (see)

auditory (hear)

kinesthetic (feel)

olfactory (smell)

gustatory (taste)

Subjective experience is directly related to our 5 senses (sub-modalities).

For example, "vision" allows us to process images, brightness, closeness, location, site, contrast, focus, as well as pictures.

We also can see with our mind's eye, as in from a memory!

Now, we have shifted from "time" to "space!" The following is a list of words and phases which communicate language shifting submodalities of space.

The following lists of words and phrases shift the submodalities of "space!"

above all
above all that
across
add more
against
aside
along side
along with
amidst
among
apart
apart from
apart of
around
ascending
aside from
aside of
back
back to

back of
behind
behind all
behind all that
all that
beside
between
beyond
across from
ascending from
bigger
blow over
bottom
bring together
clear
clear of
clear out of
closer
close down

come up
come up to
compress
condense
continue forward
disappear
disappear from
disappear to
dissolve
distance
double
double up
down
down to
draw in
drop
duplicate
expand
expand your horizons

extend

fade away

fall of

from above

from behind

from beneath

from between

front

get clear

go back

go behind

go by

go over the top

half

half way

halt

horizontal

identical

immense

in place
in place of
increase
inside
inside that
inside of
inside of that
instead of
into
keep away
keep abreast
keep going
keep going forward
keep off
leave it alone
leave it and go on
middle
missing
move forward

move ahead
move right
move right ahead
on to
open up
opposite
opposite of
opposite to
out of reach
out of the way
out
out of
outside of
overlap
overcome
overhead
past
peak
pick up

pop up
put aside
putting aside
reap
reduce
reduce in size
reduce the size
remote
repeat
repeat that (the)
replace
replace that (the)
run over
set at rest
shrink it down
side by side
smaller
somewhere to the side
split

spread out
stop
stretch
terminal point
terminate
too big
turn inside out
turn into

Note #1: Room was left for synonyms and definitions.

Note #2: In most cases, the language of "space" or shifting the submodality of space is a "verb" followed by a "preposition". You may go to a dictionary to check which words are "prepositions". I recognize the words "from" memory!

A standard English rule is: never begin or end a sentence with a preposition. In speaking, people will be confused and will not want to talk to you, if you constantly confuse them! (Just good advise)! Use this advice as a rule to live by, so as "not" to defeat your purpose "before" you even begin!

Examples: 1) You wish to rise above the situation!

2) The solution is when you can move across great distances as you rise above!

Sometimes when you are reading you might notice that someone is "adding words" to what is being written. I live in a world where when someone "adds" to language

I like to know "why" and what effect the language will have!

It's like "buyer's remorse". they tell you what they should have done, instead of what they actually "did". The word "they" is a pronoun. It could mean anybody! Or even more importantly any situation! Women are constantly doing this to men! They are always with the "wrong" guy, but when the situation ends, they always go over to "that" nice guy and say "I should have . . . etc." I don't have to finish the sentence even, because we know what they say. They made a "wrong" choice and they now want a second chance till another wrong choice comes along! If you're one of those "nice guys" do you want to be in a relationship with this type of woman? Well, let's see! She wasn't interested the first time around. She knows you're there. You must represent "financial" or "marital security" to her. Or at least till she finds another "Mr. Wrong" for "sexual gratification"!

I personally would play the game till I got the woman's phone number, and then "not" call her! She is "not" giving you a second chance. She is giving herself a second chance! Be nice about it, but know you are a "rebound" and you will get "hurt" and "burned" a second time! (If you like this woman). Always keep in mind, if you're "not" the first choice, you're the wrong choice!! (Mr. Nice Guy).

I apologize for deviating from the topic, but I have a great story to tell!

I was "not" even divorced yet, and a woman I met in a dance club/bar started to tell me an interesting story. Before she started the story, I told her I analyze handwriting, which she knew, I knew how to do, even before I started speaking to her. I saw something in a standard (loaded) sentence I asked her to write, which I did "not" tell her was in her sentence. (I read marks and strokes of writing to determine personality, traits, qualities, characteristics, and if the person has a medical problem. I am one of the top people who does this and it is a natural ability for me).

I don't know the reason why I was being so "nice and polite" to her. This was a real "bad time" in my life. What I saw in her writing was she tells "<u>lies</u>"! (Not the type of person for me!)

She communicated to me she was born with "gifts". Specifically, she is able to speak to "dead people". I said something about her "not to be speaking to dead people", and they instantly were transformed into "angels" (she changed her story) in her language! She now spoke to "angels"! I asked her if she was able to see "demons" and how many were observing us. She said, "two". I asked where are they, to which I was told they are "leaving!"

In other words "this was going nowhere fast!" The purpose of her being there, she had told me, was she should have, or was supposed to have met me "4 months earlier" (which would have been a better time). She described the place. I went into my memory as she recalled "something about an annoying woman!" Without saying nothing to her, I naturally was thinking of her! She already had it in mind to be my next wife in a long marriage. Personally, I had

had it with talking to her! (She had no credibility). I later did a card reading (tarot) at a later point in time, an extra card dropped (the "regret" card, which has a picture of a woman's face on it with tears!)

This woman had all the help of things "not" seen by a human eye, took things for granted, prepared, but not as well as was needed for a deliberate encounter, and failed to 1) create interest; 2) failed to use feminine charm; 3) communicated that I can "wait" as in wait "4 months" for her, a woman who I did not even know existed, who was not interested in me as a man, a human being or as a sex object, but as a "future", as in a later life, when she could "not" even meet me at a better point in time in my life!

Even if you know a possible future exists, it is one of many! You are "not" necessary entitled to it, but it is a possible future! What is even more important is what you do in the present, to make that possible future happen! Since the future did "not" take place yet there is possible deviations to it! The future is "not" set in stone! To improve your future you have choices. Young people go to college or trade schools to "specialize" after high school. People who "can", or have the "ability" go on to higher levels after college, as in graduate school for MBA's, law school, or medical school! Graduating usually increases credentials and earnings in later years. The armed forces in the USA will pick up the tap if you play their game by their rules, if you don't have the money and want the education!

I knew most of the people reading this are past this point, but you might have family, as in children, or nephews, cousins or even friends or their children who you can talk to about this!

The following is a list of words and phrases which affect the submodality or submodalities of time.

List of words and phrases of "time"!

abruptly
accelerate
after
ageless
all day long
already
anytime
anytime now
as
as long as
as often as
as soon as
as soon as you like
as surely as
at the same time
automatically
before

begin
beginning
beginning with
beginning of
beginning of the end
briefly
by the time that
carry through
cease
closure
come
draw to a close
conclude
consecutive
continue
continuing
continuous
delay
die out

dissolution
drag on
during
elapse
end
end of subject
end of matter
endless
every time
final stage
finale
finally
for the present
frequent
from day to day
from now
from now on
halt
here, now

here today, gone tomorrow
in due time
in the future
in the meantime
in the past
in the present
instantaneously
keep time
keep time with
last
lately
latter end
like new
live through
long awaited
look ahead
looking forward
looking forward to
look back

looking back
make time fly
mark time
marking time
meanwhile
moment by moment
future
near future
never
never ending
newness
next time
no sooner than
not now
now
often
over
over and done
over and done with

pass away
past
periodic
perpetual
perpetually
peter out
prolong
quickly
reoccurring
reoccurrence
repeat
repeating
restart
start
round the clock
run its course
sequel
sequence
short term

term
since
soon
span
speed up
stand still
still
stop
successive
suddenly
terminate
the day that
the entire time
the hour that
the month that
the year that
the time that
went that
then

thereafter

time out

time up

until

wait

want to

when

whenever

where

while

would be

yet

Examples of presuppositions of time.

1. Sooner or later you can succeed!

2. After you pause and relax you find additional energy for a long

day!

3. When you begin to study the language in this book, you begin to get better at it each and every day!

4. Before you even think about it the way you use language improves in the near future.

"Other" words and phrases which affect time and space!

List of additional words and phrases!

act out

add to the pile of

at the speed of light

bad taste

become extinct

belongs to the past

blow over

boundary
break up
bring together
brink
cancel
canceled
clear up
close
close at hand
close down
concave
convey
crack
clowning
double
duplicate
drop
edge
enduring

fade
fade away
faster
foresee
give weight to
go by
gradual
grinding to a halt
hang up
identical
immense
in the same breath
increase in tempo
increase in temperature
just around the corner
keep in mind
keep in the back of your mind
lapse
last but

leave it
leave it and go on
let it go
let go
let go of
lies ahead
limitless
lingering
look forward
looking back
look over
look out
lump together
together
make an exception
make it equal
fair
make it the same
that's fair

make no distinction
what's wrong with that
not that anything is wrong with
that!
multiply
never ending
next
next on the list
now or never
outlook
overlook
pass by
pick out
pick up
play out
quicker
release
remain
repeat

repetition
replay
restart
return to
revert to
review
see no difference
see the difference
see yourself
see for yourself
select
set at ease
settled
single
slip away
slow down
slower
sort out
sort what's important

so what's important from
what's not important
sounds the same
speed up
spinning
split
standing still
switch off
take a turn for the
the last word
tie you in knots
touch and go
turn a blind eye (to)
turn into
twinkle
two faced
two-fold
ultimate
indistinguishable

vagueness
vanish
wind up
without limit
above and beyond
working through
at once
back and forth
back away
black out
break up
bring out
bring up
carry away
close in
come together
come to mind
at any rate
at random

background
turn it around
bring up, changes, around
brush aside
aside from
carry out
center
come upon
slow down and create
the space
advance
at a stand still
at the same time
verge
breakthrough
bring down
bring forward
collapse
come to light

come to pass
come to a conclusion!

Note #1: Room is available next
to the above words for synonyms
and or definitions.

Hypnotic Time Distortion

1. When you think of the past, how far back do you want to go?

If the past is in your lifetime

A. Do you want to remember a time when . . . ?

B. Do you want to picture a time when . . . ?

Note 1: A & B are ways to time "regress" in your lifetime.

2. Do you want to travel back to a time when you did not live in this life? Like, imagining a time, when... or picturing a time when...or looking back to when. .

Note #2: 2. Is about a time before your lifetime.

3. The future did "not" happen yet, or there are several possible futures, and as time comes closer that particular version of events, or likeliness of events occurs!

A. For all practical purposes, we can imagine a time in the future.

B. But not only can we imagine a time in the future, we can also go into that future and imagine the events which will lead to this possible future.

C. But also note: for every action there is a reaction. What I mean is events are destined to go a certain way! The deviation is there, but the events are to occur. In other words: the deviation exists but the events will or are to occur. In time language "sooner or later!"

But note: We can still imagine the future, or "a possible future!"

For "Hypnotic Time Distortion"

1. Either hypnotize yourself (self-hypnosis)

2. Hypnotize someone else

A. (Preferably with their knowledge and permission).

B. (In "trust") (and with trust) (Keep the trust)!

I originally was going to end this book prior to this sentence for a number of reasons!

While I understand the "power" of the language and "hypnotic time distortion!"

A number of people reading this

information already also knows what hypnotic time distortion is and how to do it and they also understand it. Some new people to hypnosis and people who were "not" trained will "not", however, know what it is about!

The word "about" is "space" language. Like "turn about"! or "about face!"

Language has a first meaning, a second meaning, and a third meaning. When you hear the word "watch" what do you think of? (See a dictionary!)

The words "remember", "picture" and "imagine" are trance words "mental processes!"

Some people have natural

abilities powers/gifts or whatever you like to call it (help even).

Some people just imagine or "picture" things better than others!

Some other people "remember" better than others.

(Visual/auditory abilities)

When time "distortion" is used we either are hypnotizing ourselves or others.

Again, I hope with total awareness and with "good intentions" (shared benefits).

People do figure things out like: If they have been had!

Good examples of time distortion are as follows:
Example 1:

1. Bringing the better eyesight of someone forward in time from a past point in time by hypnotizing the person!

2. Applying a link and lock suggestion or more than one suggestion./(Anchor it to a common every day thing which is reoccurring on a daily basis).

Example 2:

Use technique 1 and 2 above to improve "memory" by bringing the memory when it was at the best point-in-time forward.

"Or" make the memory photographic via "pictures" like a TV set running the picture or via "sounds" like instantly playing a tape recorder of the words, phrases and sentences.

Example 3

For people with current poor minds! (etc.)

Bring their "previous minds" forward from better points in time. (Link and Lock) for best results.

These are the absolute best things to do with "time distortion!"

Yes, it can be done. For additional language on how to do it, see my book: "An Advanced Guide to Basic Hypnosis." ISBN: 0970271735. Order forms enclosed.

"Mind Reading in Written Form!"

The "Magic", "Power" and "Secrets" of "Handwriting Analysis" revealed!

By
Jeffrey Hammer

Our book can be ordered directly from us or online via a secure server from
Barnes&Nobles.com

Please print or copy this form and mail it to:
P.O. Box 314
Oceanside, NY 11572

- Price per book #4 $29.95 The Human Mind Expressed
                                              in Written Form
- Price per book #3 $89.95 Hypnosis (Basic Hypnosis)
- Price per book #2 $20.00 Mindwriting
- Price per book #1 $20.00 Mindreading in
                                              Written Form

- Shipping & Handling:* $5.00 per book
- Payment Terms: Bank Check or Money Order
- Make checks payable to: Jeffrey Hammer

Reseller and/or multiple purchase discounts available.
Contact us for details.

Orders will not be shipped until payment is received.

SHIPPING INFORMATION

Name: _____

Company Name: _____

Address: _____

Apt. or Suite: _____

City: _____

State: _____

Postal Code: _____

Country: _____

* All prices are in United States Dollars

Mind Reading in Written Form
Outline

Mindreading in written form discusses the range of human personalities and how to determine a person's emotional makeup via their handwriting. Below is an outline of the topics described in the book.

Line Traits
- Personality Slants
- Duel and multiple personalities
- Emotional personalities
- Emotionally withdrawn

Other Line Strokes
- Perfectionist
- Leadership
- Optimism
- Concentration

Zone Strokes - Mind/Body/Essence/Soul
- Lives for the moment truthfulness
- Honest
- Blunt / talkative
- Secretive
- Self deceit
- Lying

T-Strokes and D-Strokes
- Enthusiasm
- High self esteem
- Low self esteem
- Directness

- Pride & dignity-demand for respect
- Temper
- Procrastination

- Control/Umbrella
- Sarcasm/Sarcasm about self
- Domineering/Cruel
- Sensitive to criticism of of self/ideas, philosophies
- Stubborn

- Dreamer
- Sense of Humor

Mind Reading in Written Form
Outline

"M" Strokes

- Cumulative thinker
- Comprehensive thinker
- Analytical/Investigative

- Grasp of a situation
- Diplomatic
- Fear of ridicule

Lower Zone Strokes

- Fluidity of thought
- Fear of success
- Physical activity
- Sexual imagination
- Strong sex drive
- Socially selective

- Anti-social
- Physical frustration
- Aggression/anger
- Argumentative
- Jealousy

Other Items

- Desire to be needed by people
- Attention to details
- Irritation/Irritability
- Selective listener
- Desire for attention
- Desire for culture
- Persistence

- Needs a challenge
- Defiance
- Hooks & Claws
- Generosity/sharing
- Immaturity
- Excuses
- Positive attitude

From the Author

In writing *Mindreading in Written Form!*, my intention was to write the best book on the subject of handwriting analysis! I included everything on the subject which I found to be true and correct, from analyzing over two thousand peoples' handwriting. The only times I personally used psychic power, as a non-psychic person was when I analyzed the writing of people who actually had medical problems. In writing the book, I included all information which is important about analyzing a person's writing and being able to tell that person what their writing communicates about who they are! I wrote the book in an easy to understand way, so the reader can learn how to analyze handwriting, and concluded the book, so that the reader can improve their own handwriting, and personality, to become the person they want to be!

About the Author

The author has analyzed over 2000 persons' handwriting, in a two year period. The author has a large collection on books on the subject of handwriting analysis and related information. The author is currently involved in writing 3 other books, of which one will be a follow up to *Mindreading in Written Form*, the second will be a book on grammar, and the third will be an advanced language book. The author has a double bachelor's degree, master's level education, and a teaching license.

Editorial Reviews

Book Description

Mindreading in Written Form, sub-titled: The "Magic ","Power", and "Secrets" of "Handwriting Analysis" Revealed!, is the top book, and best written book on the subject of handwriting analysis / graphology! Mindreading in Written Form is excellently written, very informative, a one-hour read and the information on handwriting analysis/ graphology is made in a very easy to understand way for the reader, so that the reader can learn how to analyze a person's writing. The information that is communicated can be very useful, especially for people who have a fascination about the world and people. Reading this book will open up a whole new world of fun, a new way to read writing and enjoy the information in this book. Numerous things about the human personality are communicated in a person's writing are communicated in this book, which includes numerous and detailed pictures and diagrams allowing the reader to become an instant expert on handwriting analysis/ graphology if the reader invests the time to learn what is being explained in the book. The book communicates information about what a person's writing says about their personality, and their human qualities, in addition to a chapter on medical problems, and the concluding chapter is on how to improve your writing and "be even better"!

From the Publisher

Mindreading in Written Form! allows the non-psychic person the ability to look at someone's writing in script, like a signature and instantly know things about the person. It is also a great way to begin and hold a conversation, as well as fascinate the person you are talking to!

Mind Reading in Written Form
The Magic, Power and Secrets of Handwriting Analysis Revealed

By Jeffrey Hammer

Mind Reading in Written Form can assist you in the following ways:

- Instantly know things about the people you work with and socialize with,

- Be able to begin conversations with people about their favorite subject, themselves!

- If you are in the medical, or legal profession this book will be very useful.

- If you are an employer, or in a position of hiring individuals, the knowledge in this book will be very useful in making decisions, on who to hire.

- Instantly have more knowledge about the people you meet and deal with, just by reading this book.

This book contains the best information available on handwriting analysis in written form! Learn the secrets of Graphology. This information will enable you to know things about people by looking at their writing!

Enter the top 1% of the population that is able to do this, simply by memorizing the information in this book, a little at a time. It's very easy to learn, and you get to learn at your own pace.

This is an excellent value and an excellent resource to own. Pure power of the mind!

Mind Reading in Written Form

Table of Contents

Chapter Title

*Our book can be ordered directly from us
or online via a secure server from*
Barnes&Nobles.com

**Please print or copy this form and mail it to:
P.O. Box 314
Oceanside, NY 11572**

- Price per book #4 $29.95 The Human Mind Expressed
                                              in Written Form!
- Price per book #3 $89.95 Hypnosis (Basic Hypnosis)
- Price per book #2 $20.00 Mindwriting
- Price per book #1 $20.00 Mindreading in
                                              Written Form

- Shipping & Handling:* $5.00 per book
- Payment Terms: Bank Check or Money Order
- Make checks payable to: Jeffrey Hammer

**Reseller and/or multiple purchase discounts available.
Contact us for details.**

Orders will not be shipped until payment is received.

SHIPPING INFORMATION

Name: _____

Company Name: _____

Address: _____

Apt. or Suite: _____

City: _____

State: _____

Postal Code: _____

Country: _____

* All prices are in United States Dollars

"MINDWRITING"!

Improving your personality,
traits, qualities, characteristics,
and your writing with
handwriting analysis and
affirmations!

By the author of
"Mind Reading in Written Form!"
Jeffrey Hammer

In my first book on the subject of handwriting analysis titled, Mind Reading in Written Form! I communicated expert knowledge in teaching people to analyze handwriting and to discover an individual's personality, traits, qualities, and characteristics.

The concluding chapter of Mind Reading in Written Form is titled "Fixing It!" In the last chapter I gave some tips on how to improve and change things in writing to improve a person's personality for the better. To improve things in writing!

"Mindwriting"!
Improving your personality, traits, qualities, characteristics,
and your writing with handwriting analysis and affirmations!
By Jeffrey Hammer

Editorial Review

Book Description

"Mindwriting" continues where *Mind Reading in Written Form!*" concludes, which is "Fixing it!" "Mindwriting" shows you numerous ways to improve your personality, traits, qualities, characteristics, and your writing by applying handwriting analysis and affirmations, and by showing you better ways to write in script, as well as in print. "Mindwriting," like *Mind Reading in Written Form!*, also explains how to analyze handwriting. While *Mind Reading in Written Form!* is a picture book that teaches how to analyze a person's handwriting, and to do handwriting analysis, "Mindwriting" is a self-improvement book. "Mindwriting" is more like a detailed explanation book which compliments and supplements "Mind Reading in Written Form!," and is also the follow-up book to *Mind Reading in Written Form!*" More clarity is added to allow the reader additional enhancement and to improve and make the reader more skilled, and to allow the reader to improve on a very real human level! Not only are these two of the best books on handwriting analysis, they are two of the best books ever written!

From the Publisher

All the information that you can possibly ever want on handwriting analysis is available in this book! "Mindwriting" includes excellent information on improving your personality and writing in one book! This is the book with the best information on self-improvement ever written, and it is written in a very reader-friendly way! The book shows you how to improve your personality, traits, qualities, characteristics, and your writing, and has much, much more very important and real-life relevant information in it! The book is excellently and very brilliantly written! "Mindwriting" shows numerous ways to improve your writing and your personality by making simple, easy changes in small items in your writing. "Mindwriting" gets exceptionally very high marks for having excellent, and the very best information in it! Highly recommended! A must buy!

From the Author

I set out to write the very best self-improvement book ever written using handwriting analysis, and affirmations, to show people how to improve their personality, traits, qualities, characteristics, writing, and I included a lot of other important information about people, and processing of information from the mind to paper in writing. I included honest, accurate, relevant, and important and detailed information in this book! The best information, and value! I included ways to become more honest, more detailed, ways to improve memory, raise-self-esteem, enthusiasm, and excitement, and other numerous, interesting and fascinating information like what a person's eyes say!

About the Author

Jeffrey Hammer has masters level college education, a teaching license, experience in teaching and experience working in the business world. Jeffrey Hammer in the author and the publisher of the book "Mind Reading in Written Form!," and he is currently writing the first of three advanced language books!

Mindwriting is brilliantly written!

Reviewer: A reader from U.SA.

All the information you ever wanted to possibly learn about "handwriting analysis" and excellent information on improving your writing and personality all in one book! This is the best information on self-improvement ever written! If you ever just wanted to look at someone's writing, and see how their mind worked, this is the book to read! Jeffrey Hammer, not only shows you how to improve people's personalities, traits, qualities and characteristics, but also, what the writing says, and how to change the writing, to be an even better person! "Mindwriting", definitely continues where Jeffrey Hammer's *Mind Reading in Written Form!*", concludes "fixing it". Changing for the better, and self-improvement! While *Mind Reading in Written Form!*" is "excellently written!", "Mindwriting", is "brilliantly" written! Both books teach you how to analyze a person's writing! "Mindwriting" also shows the numerous things communicated in writing, which you can improve on, to change your personality! Examples would be: 1. raising self-esteem, 2. Improving memory, 3. becoming more detailed, and also numerous other ways to improve yourself, by simply changing a small item in the way you write on a conscious level! Not only does the book: "Mindwriting" get high marks, but it is also absolutely brilliant"!!!

EDITORIAL REVIEWS:

<u>Book Descriptions</u>:

An Advanced Guide to Basic Hypnosis"! is just that! "An Introduction to the "Power of Hypnosis"! If you ever wanted to learn "hypnosis", in a safe way, with "warnings" and "advice", you now have one of the best books written on how to learn it with the information that you want to learn, to actually understand the meanings of what hypnosis, "is", what hypnosis, "does" and how hypnosis affects people! The book includes: "weasel phrases", "trance words", hypnotic definitions, words related to hypnosis and mental process, as well as dictionary definitions to expand and define meanings as to word usages! Supplementary information to enhance and compliment the core information, is also included! Warnings as to what "not" to do, as well as suggestions to improve on a real human level are included! Clear definitions and excellent indexes are in this book! The book has "good advice", "good information", and very good "suggestions!" The purpose of the book is to "improve", "enhance", and amplify the "good!" The book falls somewhere between a dictionary and reference book on what basic hypnosis is, how to define it, as well as the meaning of basic hypnotic language. An excellent book for beginners. An excellent reference book!

An Advanced Guide to "Basic Hypnosis"

By the author of
"Mind Reading in Written Form!"
and "Mindwriting" (Improving Your Personality)

Jeffrey Hammer

From the Publisher

All the information that you can possibly ever want on "Basic Hypnosis" plus extras are included in this book! Excellent information! The best information! Including real life relevant information. The book is very knowledgeable, and informative! This book gets excellent marks for top information! Highly recommended!

From the Author

In writing "An Advanced Guide to Basic Hypnosis!", my intention was to write one of the best introduction books to Hypnosis!" I included every definition to everything ever related to the words, meanings, and definitions of basic hypnosis and basic hypnotic language! I included everything that is important to understanding what basic hypnosis "is", what it "does", and excellent advice and suggestions on what "not" to do as well as what to do to get the most out of this book!

About the Author

The author: Jeffrey Hammer has been doing advanced hypnosis a number of years. Jeffrey Hammer is the author of: 1. "Mind Reading in Written Form!" and 2. "Mindwriting" improving your personality traits, qualities, characteristics, and writing with handwriting analysis and affirmations! Jeffrey Hammer has analyzed over 3000 samples of handwriting over a several year period and is one of the top people int he country who does handwriting analysis/graphology and has written 2 of the top book on the subject of handwriting analysis! Jeffrey Hammer has masters level education. Experience working in the business world, and experience in teaching. JeffreyHammer is currently writing a grammar book which will be followed by an advanced language book!

Index

Outline

1. Introduction:

1A. The reasons as to why I am writing this book.

1B. The subject and affect of hypnosis.

1C. What hypnosis does.

1D. Resisting and redefining the language.

1E. Who knows and does hypnosis.

1F. The age of information, the internet and information on hypnosis being easily available.

2. Warning and Disclaimer #1.

2A. Don't get started!

2B. Altering your personal mental state.

2C. Just looking after your personal well being.

4A. Just to review warning and disclaimer #1.

4B. Just to review warning and disclaimer #2.

4C. Misuse of power.

4D. Examples of misuse of language and consequences of actions.

4E. Create and invent!

5. Words related to mental processes.

5A. A suggestible, idea, mental, mend, mind, normal, dream sleep.

5B. Dictionary definition which are applicable.

5C. A guide to basic hypnosis.

5D. Hypnosis defined.

5E. Hypnotic defined.

5F. Trance defined.

5G. Suggestion/Suggest: defined

Our book can be ordered directly from us or online via a secure server from Barnes&Nobles.com

Please print or copy this form and mail it to:
P.O. Box 314
Oceanside, NY 11572

- **Price per book #4** $29.95 **The Human Mind Expressed in Written Form!**
- **Price per book #3** $89.95 **Hypnosis (Basic Hypnosis)**
- **Price per book #2** $20.00 **Mindwriting**
- **Price per book #1** $20.00 **Mindreading in Written Form**

- **Shipping & Handling:*** $5.00 **per book**
- **Payment Terms:**   **Bank Check or Money Order**
- **Make checks payable to:**   **Jeffrey Hammer**

Reseller and/or multiple purchase discounts available.
Contact us for details.

Orders will not be shipped until payment is received.

SHIPPING INFORMATION

Name: _____

Company Name: _____

Address: _____

Apt. or Suite: _____

City: _____

State: _____

Postal Code: _____

Country: _____

* All prices are in United States Dollars

144

"MINDWRITING"!

Improving your personality, traits, qualities, characteristics, and your writing with handwriting analysis and affirmations!

By the author of
"Mind Reading in Written Form!"
Jeffrey Hammer

"Mindwriting II"

From the Publisher

All the information that you can possibly ever want on handwriting analysis is available in this book! "Mindwriting" includes excellent information on improving your personality and writing in one book! This is the book with the best information on self-improvement ever written, and it is written in a very reader-friendly way! The book shows you how to improve your personality, traits, qualities, characteristics, and your writing, and has much, much more very important and real-life relevant information in it! The book is excellently and very brilliantly written! "Mindwriting" shows numerous ways to improve your writing and your personality by making simple, easy changes in small items in your writing. "Mindwriting" gets exceptionally very high marks for having excellent, and the very best information in it! Highly recommended! A must buy!

From the Author

I set out to write the very best self-improvement book ever written using handwriting analysis, and affirmations, to show people how to improve their personality, traits, qualities, characteristics, writing, and I included a lot of other important information about people, and processing of information from the mind to paper in writing. I included honest, accurate, relevant, and important and detailed information in this book! The best information, and value! I included ways to become more honest, more detailed, ways to improve memory, raise-self-esteem, enthusiasm, and excitement, and other numerous, interesting and fascinating information like what a person's eyes say!

About the Author

Jeffrey Hammer has masters level college education, a teaching license, experience in teaching and experience working in the business world. Jeffrey Hammer is the author and the publisher of the book "Mind Reading in Written Form!," and he is currently writing the first of three advanced language books! Jeffrey Hammer has also analyzed over 3,000 writing samples.

Mindwriting II is brilliantly written!

Reviewer: A reader from U.SA.

All the information you ever wanted to possibly learn about "handwriting analysis" and excellent information on improving your writing and personality all in one book! This is the best information on self-improvement ever written! If you ever just wanted to look at someone's writing, and see how their mind worked, this is the book to read! Jeffrey Hammer, not only shows you how to improve people's personalities, traits, qualities and characteristics, but also, what the writing says, and how to change the writing, to be an even better person! "Mindwriting", definitely continues where Jeffrey Hammer's *Mind Reading in Written Form!*", concludes "fixing it". Changing for the better, and self-improvement! While *Mind Reading in Written Form!*" is "excellently written!", "Mindwritng", is "brilliantly" written! Both books teach you how to analyze a person's writing! "Mindwriting" also shows the numerous things communicated in writing, which you can improve on, to change your personality! Examples would be: 1. raising self-esteem, 2. Improving memory, 3. becoming more detailed, and also numerous other ways to improve yourself, by simply changing a small item in the way you write on a conscious level! Not only does the book: "Mindwriting" get high marks, but it is also absolutely brilliant"!!!

"Mindwriting II"!
Improving your personality, traits, qualities, characteristics,
and your writing with handwriting analysis and affirmations!
By Jeffrey Hammer

Editorial Review

Book Description

"Mindwriting" continues where *"Mind Reading in Written Form!"* concludes, which is "Fixing it!" "Mindwriting" shows you numerous ways to improve your personality, traits, qualities, characteristics, and your writing by applying handwriting analysis and affirmations, and by showing you better ways to write in script, as well as in print. "Mindwriting," like *"Mind Reading in Written Form!*, also explains how to analyze handwriting. While *"Mind Reading in Written Form!* is a picture book that teaches how to analyze a person's handwriting, and to do handwriting analysis, "Mindwriting" is a self-improvement book. "Mindwriting" is more like a detailed explanation book which compliments and supplements "Mind Reading in Written Form!," and is also the follow-up book to *"Mind Reading in Written Form!"* More clarity is added to allow the reader additional enhancement and to improve and make the reader more skilled, and to allow the reader to improve on a very real human level! Not only are these two of the best books on handwriting analysis, they are two of the best books ever written!

Table of Contents

Outline

1. Introduction "Parts": I, II, III
2. Affirmations
2A. Affirming the positive!
2B. Sleep learning
2C. Why "try" when you can succeed!
2D. Sleeping for solutions
3. Improving line strokes
3A. Perfection, but "not" excess
4A. Leadership
4B. Optimism and improving it
4C. Concentration
4D. Attention spans/listening
4E. Communication/focus
4F. Selective listener

6S. "U's" into "V's" and "V's" into "U's"

6T. Analytica/Investigative

6U. Garland style writing

6V. "N's" into "U's"

6W. Grasp of a situation

6X. Being more diplomatic

6Y. "Thread styles of writing"

6Z. "Cautious decisionmakers!"

6AA. "Cautious/minimum risk"

6BB. Diplomatic

6CC. Fear of ridicule

6DD. Being less likely to be laughed at

6EE. Jealousy

6FF. Becoming less jealous

6GG. Less need to be needed

Zone Strokes
Mind/Body/Essence/Soul

8A. Lives for the moment

8B. Egos - large, healthy & weak

8C. "Spur" of the moment

8D. Thinking about the future

8E. Eliminating premature and bad choices

8F. Staying away from trouble and staying out of trouble

8G. Things to consider

8H. Medical zones in writing

8I. Medical problem revealed in writing

8J. Improving and affirmations

8K. Medical problems revisited

8L. Mind, body.

8M. A dent to the "left".

8N. Head injuries & medical problems

8O. Fatigue

8P. Erratic writing/nervous tension/dishonesty/stroke

8Q. Arthritis

9. The "Lower Zone!"

Lower Zone Strokes

9A. Fluidity of thought

9B. Increasing fluidity of thought

9C. Increasing imagination and creativity

9D. Increasing success

9E. Physical activity

9F. Sexual imagination

9G. Strong sex drive

9H. Fear of success

9I. Socially selective

9J. Increasing trust, friends and friendship

9K. Anti-social

9L. Physical frustration

9M. Losing physical frustration

9N. Aggression/anger

9O. Letting anger go/letting anger pass/losing anger

9P. Controlling aggressiveness

9Q. Desire for attention

9R. Decreasing the need for attention

9S. Perversion in writing

10. Improving T's and D's

10A. Reviewing i qualities found in "t's"

10B. Dreamer

10C. Procrastination - also in i & t
10D. Temper
10E. Stubborness in letter "t"
10F. Directness
10G. Getting to the point
10H. Reciprocality
10I. Pride, dignity and respect
10J. Vanity/ "real world" perception
10K. Pride & dignity - demand for respect
10L. T-Strokes and D-Strokes
10M. Control/Umbrella
10N. Excuses
10O. Excuses and the ability to stop making excuses
10P. Domineering

10Q. Dominating a situation vs. being equal

10R. Cruelty

10S. Cruelty vs. lack of cruelty

10T. Positive attitude

10U. Positive attitude

10V. Sarcasm/Sarcasm about self

10W. From sarcasm to being positive

10X. Sarcasm about self and fixing it

10Y. Sensitive to criticism of self (d) / ideas, philosophies (t)

10Z. Lessening sensitivity to criticism of self

10AA. Lessening sensitivity to criticism of ideas and philosophies

10BB. Sense of humor

10CC. Jealousy to eliminating jealousy.

10DD. Persistence or less persistence.

10EE. Enthusiasm

10FF. High self esteem

10GG. Low self esteem

11. Other writing items and strokes

"Other Strokes"

"Other Items"

11A. . The desire for culture

11B. Needs a challenge

11C. Challenge worthy to lessening the need to be challenged

11D. Defiance and writing letters correctly

11E. Hooks and Claws and learning to let go

11Q. Ending a sentence with a period.

11R. Looking over your writing

12. Personalities

12A. A story about dual personalities and models of the world

12B. One or more personalities

12C. Dual and multiple personalities

12D. The writing slant

12E. Three faces of Eve/16 faces of Sybil!

12F. Line Taits

    1. Personality Slants Exhibit 1 & 2

    2. Dual and Multiple Personalities -

164

The "Human Mind" "Expressed" in "Written Form!"

"MINDWRITING" II

Even more improvement of personality, traits, qualities, characteristics, and writing!

By

Jeffrey Hammer

The "Human Mind" "Expressed" in "Written Form!"

"Mindwriting II"
Improving your personality, traits, qualities, characteristics, and your writing with handwriting analysis and affirmatoins!
By Jeffrey Hammer

Editorial Review

Book Description:
The Human Mind Expressed in Written Form!!

"Mindwriting II" continues where "Mind Reading in Written Form!" and "Mindwriting" concludes which is it:shows you numerous ways to improve your personality, traits, qualities, characteristics, and your writing by applying handwriting analysis and affirmations, and by showing you better ways to write in script, as well as in print! This book teaches how to analyze a person's handwriting, and to do handwriting analysis, "Mindwriting II" is a self-improvement book! "Mindwriting II" is more like a detailed explanation book which compliments and supplements "Mind Reading in Written Form!," and Mindwriting and combines both into one book. The book is combined and additions are added to enhance clarity to allow the reader additional enhancement and to improve on a very real human level! Not only is this one of the best books on handwriting analysis, it is the best book ever written on handwriting analysis and self-improvement!

> ## THE "HUMAN MIND" "EXPRESSED" IN "WRITTEN FORM!"
>
> ### "MINDWRITING" II
> *Even more improvement of personality, traits, qualities, characteristics, and writing!*
>
> By
> Jeffrey Hammer

Our book can be ordered directly from us or online via a secure server from Barnes&Nobles.com

Please print or copy this form and mail it to:
P.O. Box 314
Oceanside, NY 11572

- **Price per book #4** $29.95 The Human Mind Expressed in Written Form!
- **Price per book #3** $89.95 Hypnosis (Basic Hypnosis)
- **Price per book #2** $20.00 Mindwriting
- **Price per book #1** $20.00 Mindreading in Written Form

- **Shipping & Handling:*** $5.00 per book
- **Payment Terms:**   Bank Check or Money Order
- **Make checks payable to:** Jeffrey Hammer

Reseller and/or multiple purchase discounts available.
Contact us for details.

Orders will not be shipped until payment is received.

SHIPPING INFORMATION

Name: _____

Company Name: _____

Address: _____

Apt. or Suite: _____

City: _____

State: _____

Postal Code: _____

Country: _____

* All prices are in United States Dollars

"Mind Reading in Written Form!"

The "Magic", "Power" and "Secrets" of "Handwriting Analysis" revealed!

By
Jeffrey Hammer

An Advanced Guide to "Basic Hypnosis"

By the author of
"Mind Reading in Written Form!"
and "Mindwriting" (Improving Your Personality

Jeffrey Hammer

The "Human Mind" "Expressed" in "Written Form!"

"MINDWRITING" II

Even more improvement of personality, traits, qualities, characteristics, and writing!

By

Jeffrey Hammer

Our book can be ordered directly from us or online via a secure server from
Barnes&Nobles.com

Please print or copy this form and mail it to:
P.O. Box 314
Oceanside, NY 11572

- Price per book #4 $29.95 **The Human Mind Expressed**
                                      in Written Form
- Price per book #3 $89.95 **Hypnosis (Basic Hypnosis)**
- Price per book #2 $20.00 **Mindwriting**
- Price per book #1 $20.00 **Mindreading in**
                                      Written Form

- **Shipping & Handling:*** $5.00 per book
- **Payment Terms:**   **Bank Check or Money Order**
- **Make checks payable to:**   **Jeffrey Hammer**

Reseller and/or multiple purchase discounts available.
Contact us for details.

Orders will not be shipped until payment is received.

SHIPPING INFORMATION

Name: _____

Company Name: _____

Address: _____

Apt. or Suite: _____

City: _____

State: _____

Postal Code: _____

Country: _____

* All prices are in United States Dollars

Editorial Reviews

Book Description:
Transcending Time and Space! Hypnotic Time Distortion! is an advance hypnosis book which includes out-of-body experiences and NLP. The book has 4 sections: Part 1, the introduction, is about OBE's. Part 2 is about NLP how people process and communicate language (the senses). Part 3 of the book is all about "time" and "space" language, temporary and permanent language and "reference" to words, phrases, and comments which communicate "time" and "space". Part 4 of the book is "Hypnotic Time Distortion!" How people use mental processes to relate to the past and future from the present. Examples are given on how to use time distortion for self-improvement. Excellent example on improving memory is included!

From the Author

In writing "Transcending Time and Space", it was my intention to write one of the best reference books on "time" and "space" language! I also wanted to give excellent suggestions and advice to "help people" by showing how to use "hypnotic time distortion" for self-improvement!

About the Author

This is Jeffrey Hammer's fifth book! Jeffrey Hammer has written five books in a three year period! Jeffrey Hammer is the author of: 1) "Mind Reading in Written Form!; 2) "Mindwriting"; 3) "The Human Mind Expressed in Written Form"; and 4) "An Advanced Guide to Basic Hypnosis!" Jeffrey Hammer is also one of the top people in the USA and the world who does handwriting analysis (graphology)! Jeffrey Hammer has analyzed over 3,000 people's samples of writing and has written three top books on Handwriting Analysis! Jeffrey Hammer's first hypnosis book is a reference book and is "one of a kind!" Jeffrey Hammer also does "basic palmistry"! Jeffrey Hammer has Master's level education, has worked in teaching, and also in the business world. Look forward to Jeffrey Hammer's "next book!"